Z PIR
Pirotta, Saviour.
Hey riddle riddle!
95614397

Copyright © 1989 Saviour Pirotta
Illustrations © 1989 Nancy Hellen
First published 1989 by Blackie and Son Ltd

All rights reserved. No part of this publication may be reproduced, stored in a retrieval system, or transmitted in any form or by any means, electronic, mechanical, photocopying, recording or otherwise without the written permission of the Publishers.

British Library Cataloguing in Publication Data

Pirotta, Saviour, *1958–*
Hey, riddle riddle!
I. Title
823[F]
ISBN 0-216-92651-3

Blackie and Son Ltd
7 Leicester Place
London WC2H 7BP

First American edition published in 1989 by
Peter Bedrick Books
2112 Broadway, Rm. #318
New York NY 10023

Library of Congress Cataloging-in-Publication Data

Pirotta, Saviour.
    Hey riddle riddle!
    Summary: Six guessing riddles depict an animal on one page and the answer on the next page.
    1. Riddle, Juvenile. [1. Riddles, 2. Animals]
I. Hellen, Nancy. II. Title.
PN6371.5.P57   1989   823'.91402   88-34356
ISBN 0-87226-408-4

Printed in Hong Kong

Hey Riddle Riddle!

Saviour Pirotta & Nancy Hellen

Blackie
London

Bedrick/Blackie
New York

I've eaten corn
since I was born.

Sometimes I fly
but not too high.
Who am I?

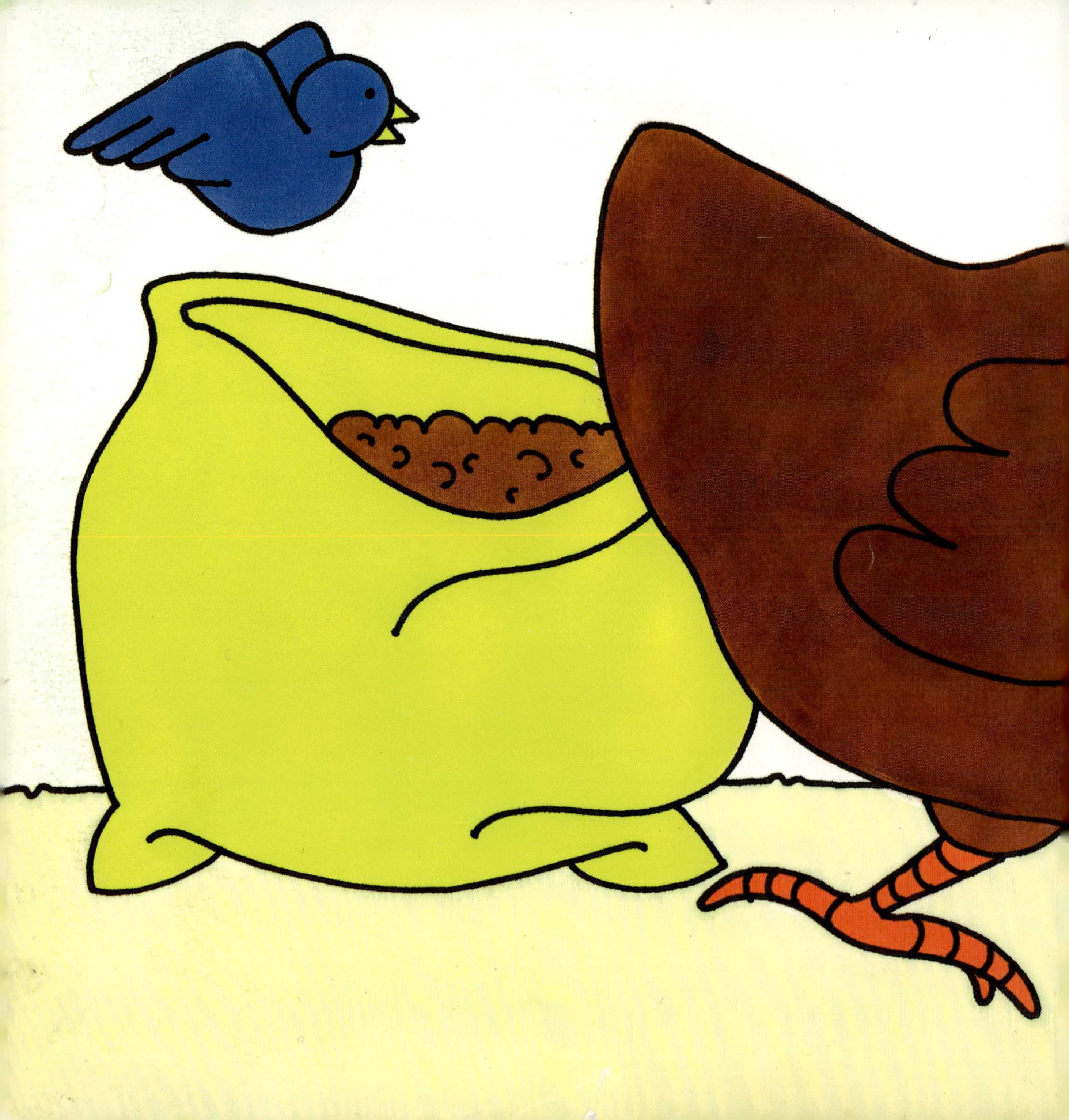

The hen.

I sleep by day
and fly by night.

I cannot sing
but I can bite.
Who am I?

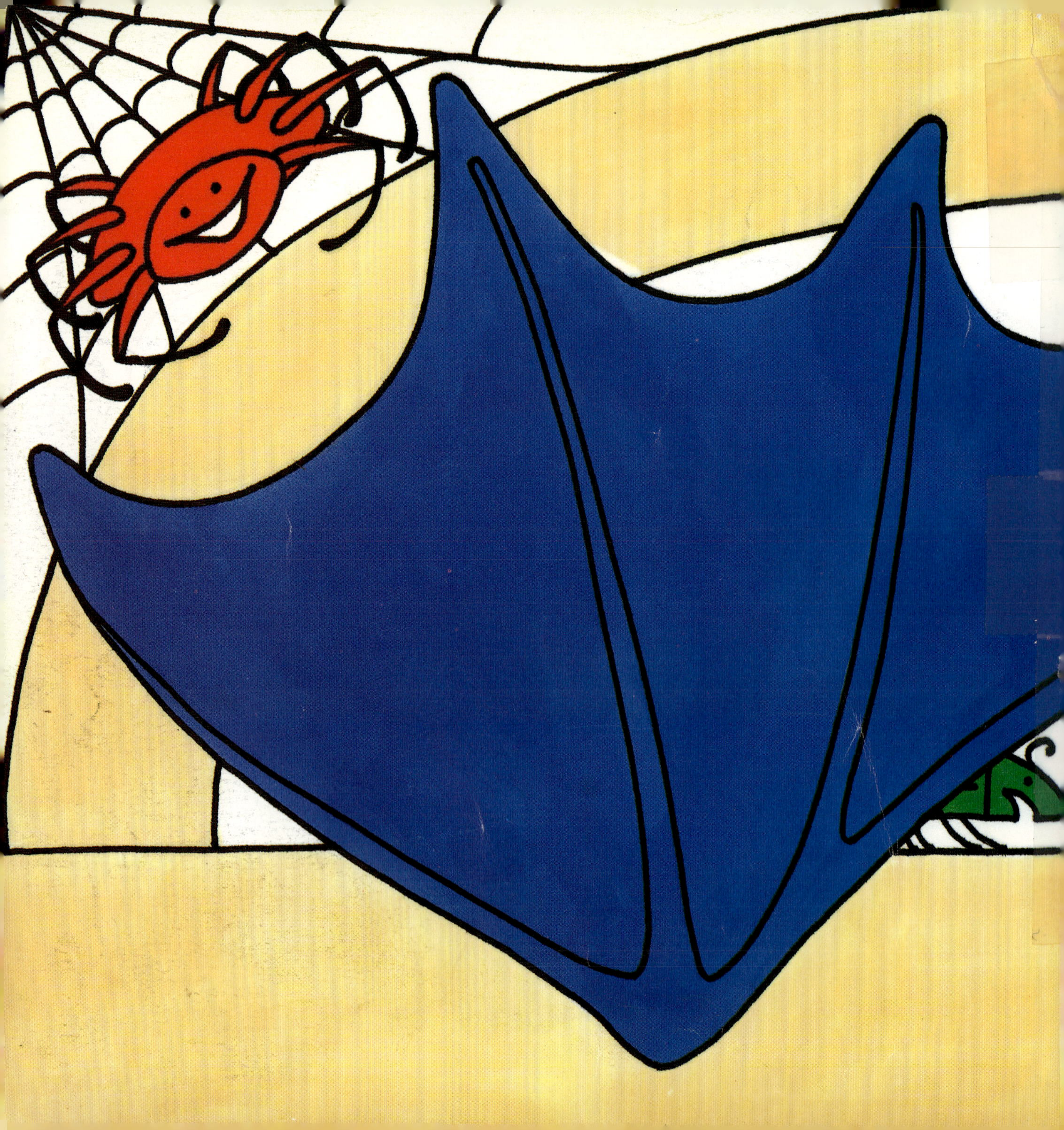

The bat.

My house is brown
with rings of blue.

And when I move
my house moves too.
Who am I?

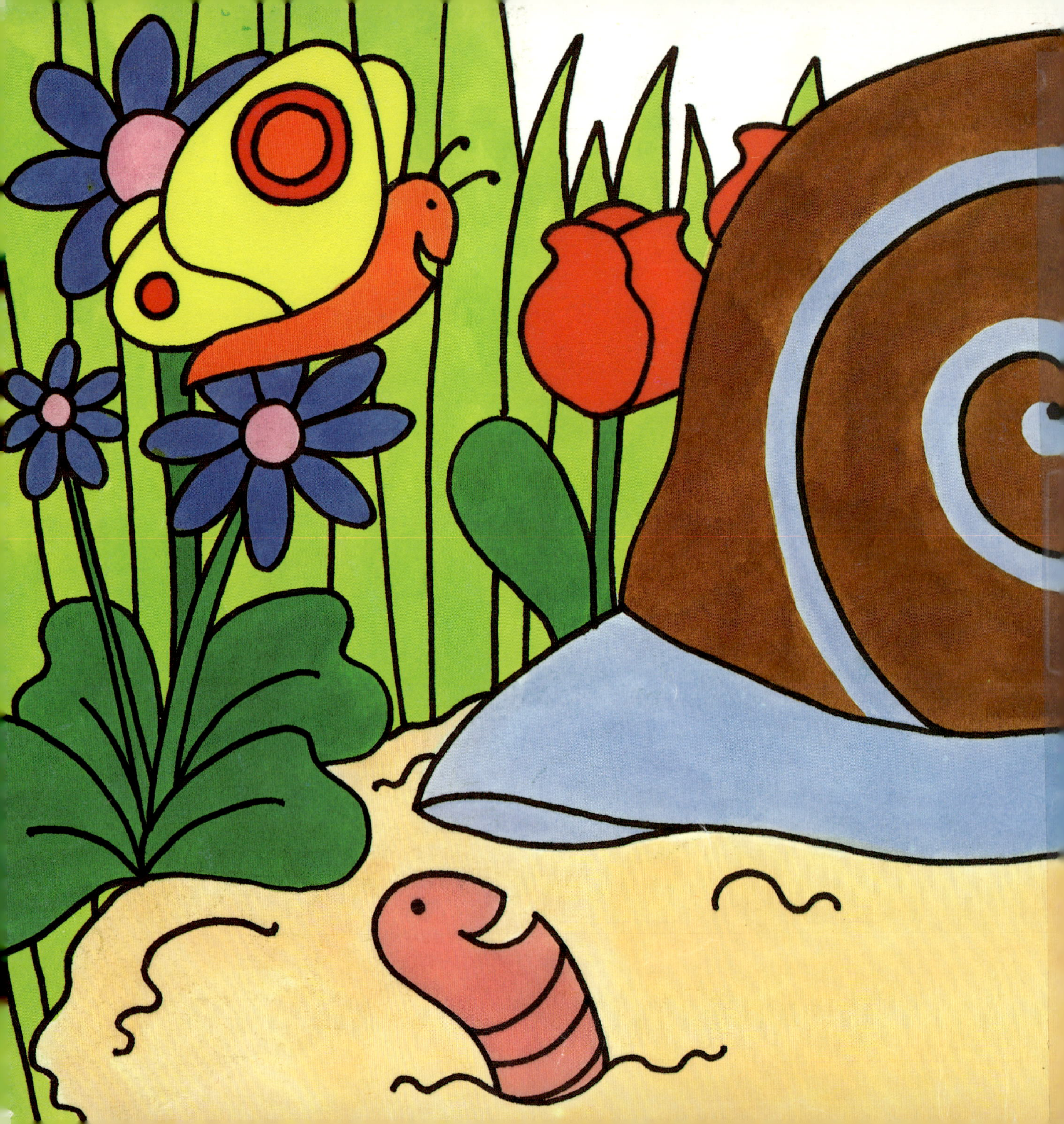

The snail.

My house is deep
on the sea bed.

I have eight legs
but just one head.
Who am I?

The octopus.

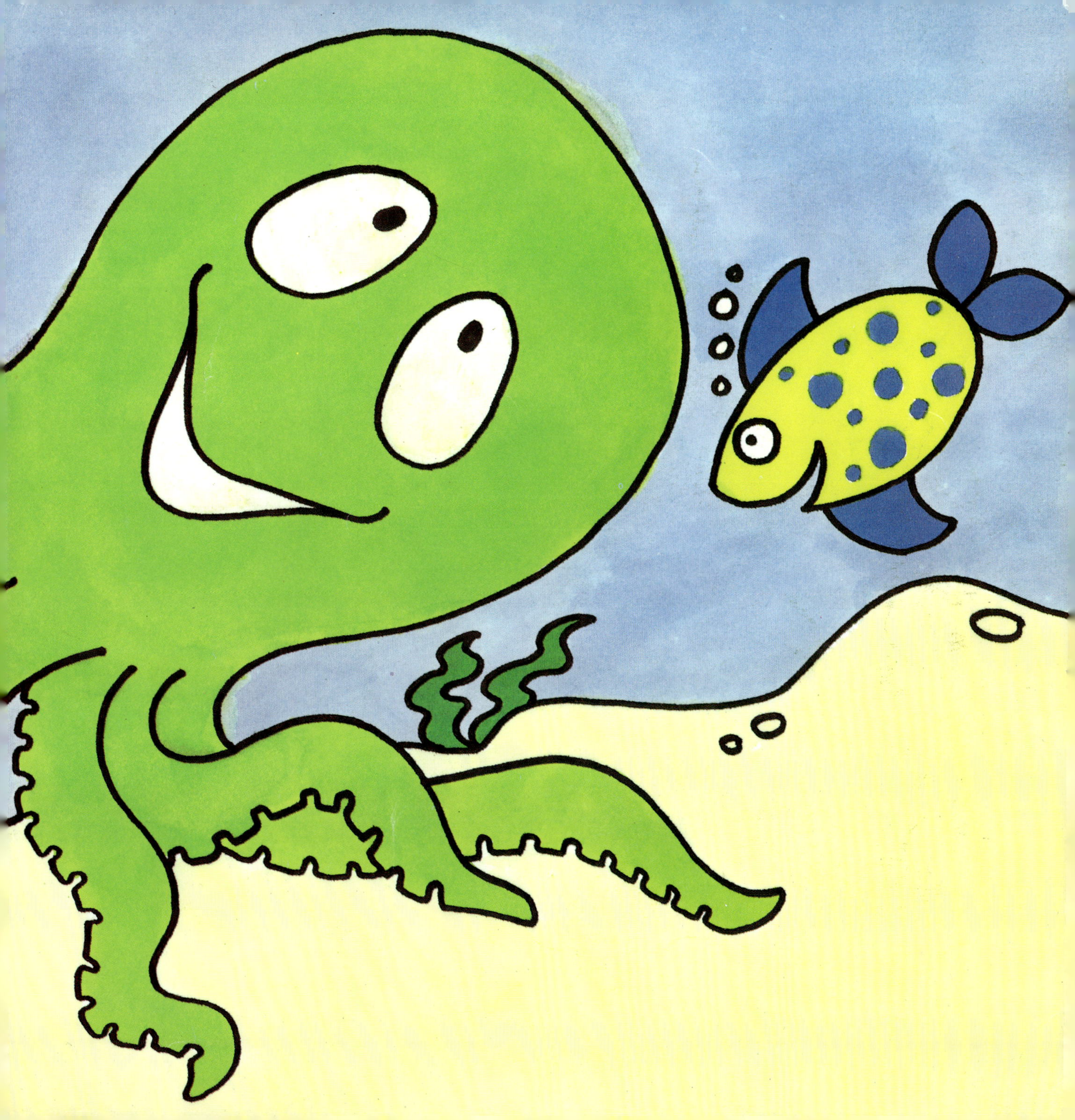

I creep along
the kitchen shelf.

although grey mice
taste just as nice.
Who am I?

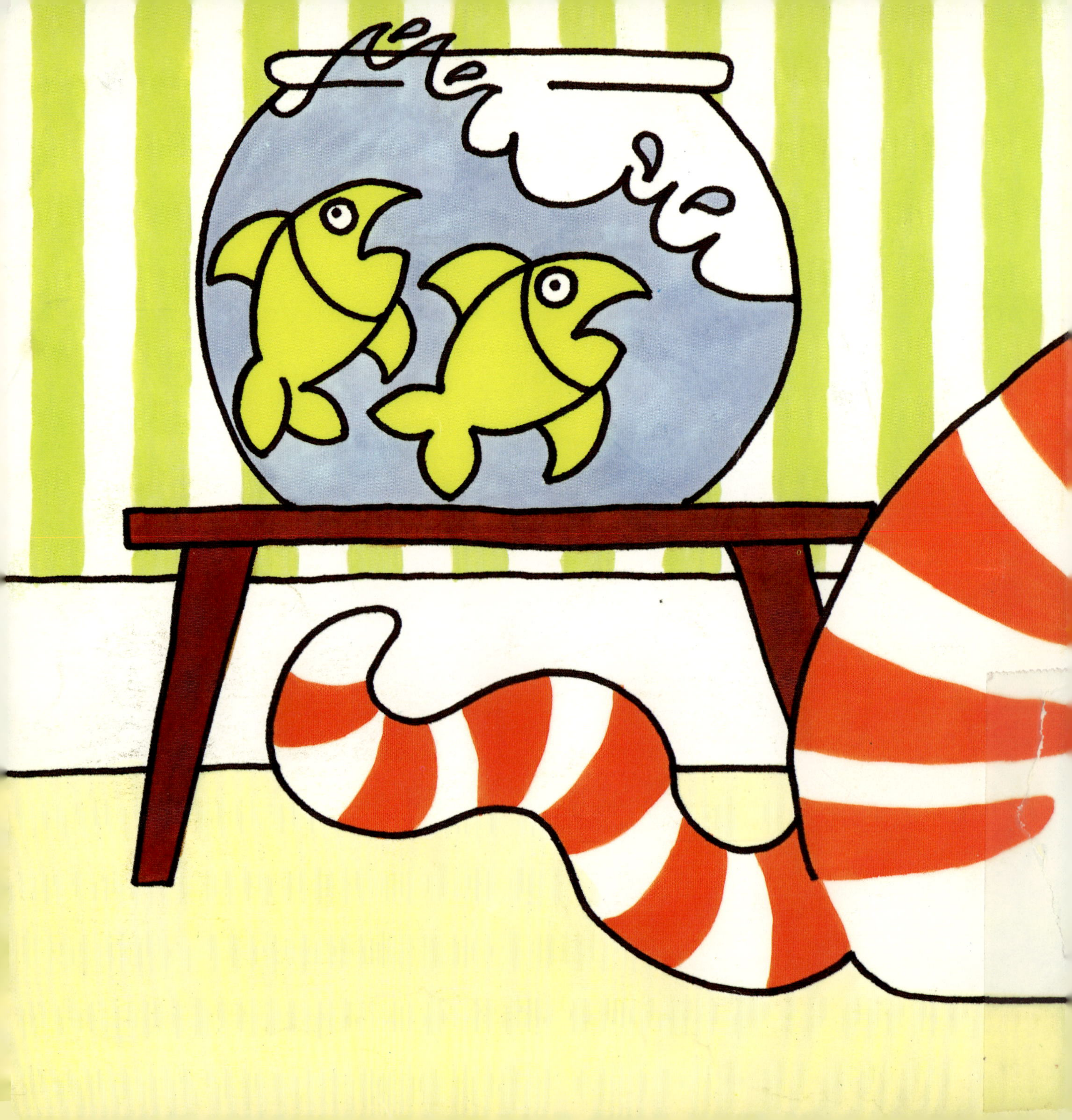

The cat.

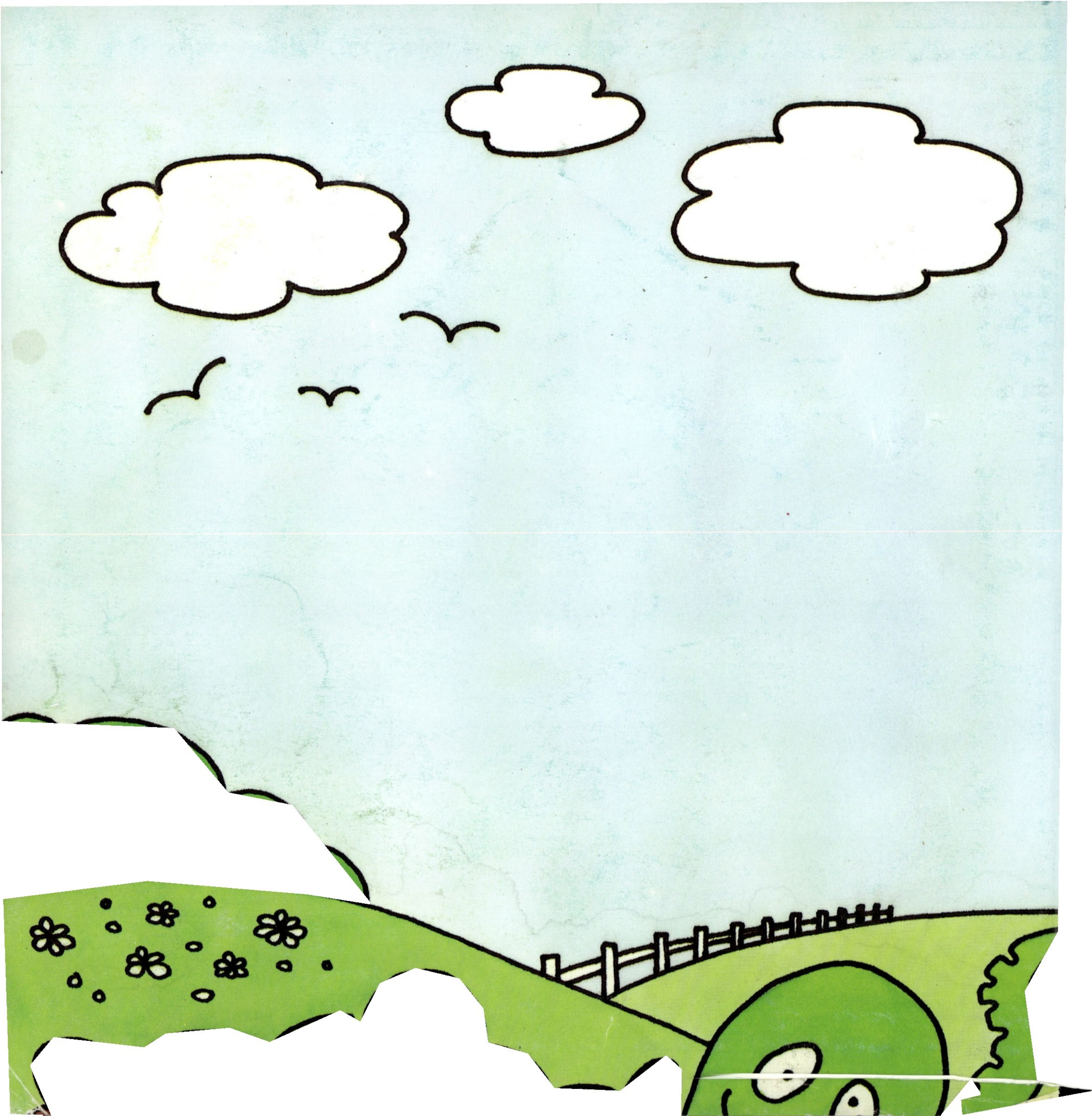